GLOW IN THE DARK
BOOK OF
OCEAN
CREATURES

Published in the United States in 2002 by The Millbrook Press, Inc.,
2 Old New Milford Road, Brookfield, Connecticut 06804

Created and produced by Nicholas Harris and Claire Aston,
Orpheus Books Ltd.

Illustrated by Elisabetta Ferrero, Mariano Valsesia, and Gary Hincks

Consultant: Professor Peter Herring,
Southampton Oceanography Centre, UK

Copyright © 2002 Orpheus Books Ltd.

Library of Congress Cataloging-in-Publication Data

Harris, Nicholas, 1956-
     Glow in the dark book of ocean creatures / [Nicholas Harris ; illustrated by Elisabetta
Ferrero, Mariano Valsesia, and Gary Hincks].
          p. cm.
     Summary: A glow-in-the-dark introduction to the variety of animals living at various
depths in the world's oceans.
     ISBN 0-7613-1495-4
     1. Marine animals--Juvenile literature. 2. Ocean--Juvenile literature. 3.
Glow-in-the-dark books--Specimens. [1. Marine animals. 2. Ocean. 3. Glow-in-the-dark
books. 4. Toy and movable books.] I. Ferrero, Elisabetta, ill. II. Valsesia, Mariano, ill.
III. Hincks, Gary, ill.

QL122.2 .H3667 2002
591.77--dc21   2001044161

Printed and bound in China

1 3 5 4 2

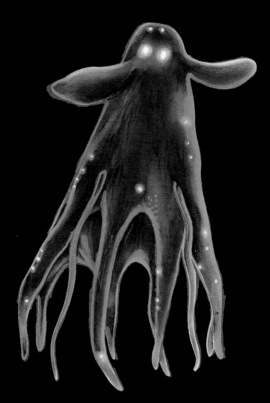

GLOW IN THE DARK
BOOK OF
OCEAN
CREATURES

written by
Nicholas Harris

illustrated by
Elisabetta Ferrero, Mariano Valsesia, and Gary Hincks

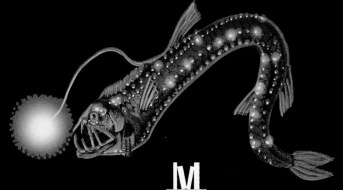

M
The Millbrook Press
Brookfield, Connecticut

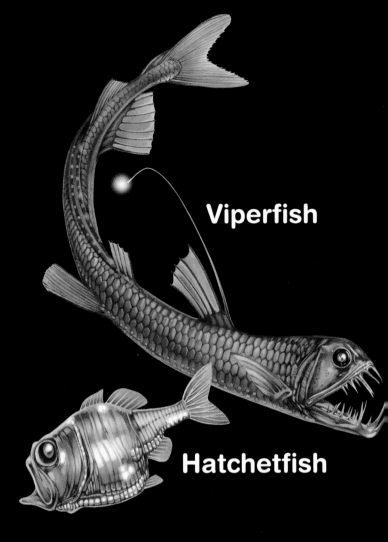

Viperfish

Hatchetfish

Firefly squid

CONTENTS

THE OCEANS cover more than two thirds of the Earth's surface. They are home to millions of different kinds of animals. Most live in the shallow coastal waters where there is plenty of food. Some ocean creatures live at greater depths, however. They feed on dead animals or plants that rain down from the waters above—or on each other. The deep oceans are cold and black. To see, or to lure their prey toward them, these deepwater animals create their own light. This is called bioluminescence.

Some of these glowing creatures are also glowing in the pages of this book. For the pages with special glow-in-the-dark text and illustrations, look for the blue corner squares. Hold the book open at any one of these pages under a light for twenty seconds or so, then turn out the light.

Gulper eel

ABOUT THIS BOOK

MOST ocean creatures live close to the water's surface. During the day, sunlight reaches down through the water. Here, tiny plants and animals, called plankton, provide a rich source of food. Below about 650 feet there is very little light. The few animals that live here must survive on dead plants and animals that sink down from above. Many deepwater animals are able to produce light from their own bodies. They glow in the dark!

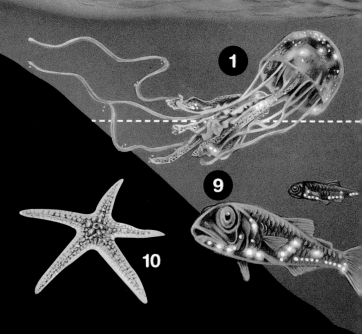

1   Jellyfish
2   Black star-eater
3   Flashlight fish
4   Plankton
5   Hatchetfish
6   Black dragonfish
7   Shrimp
8   Loosejaw
9   Lantern fish
10 Starfish
11 Deep-sea squid
12 Viperfish
13 Red comb jelly
14 Vampire squid
15 Deep-sea anglerfish
16 Gulper eel

WHO GLOWS IN THE OCEAN DEPTHS?

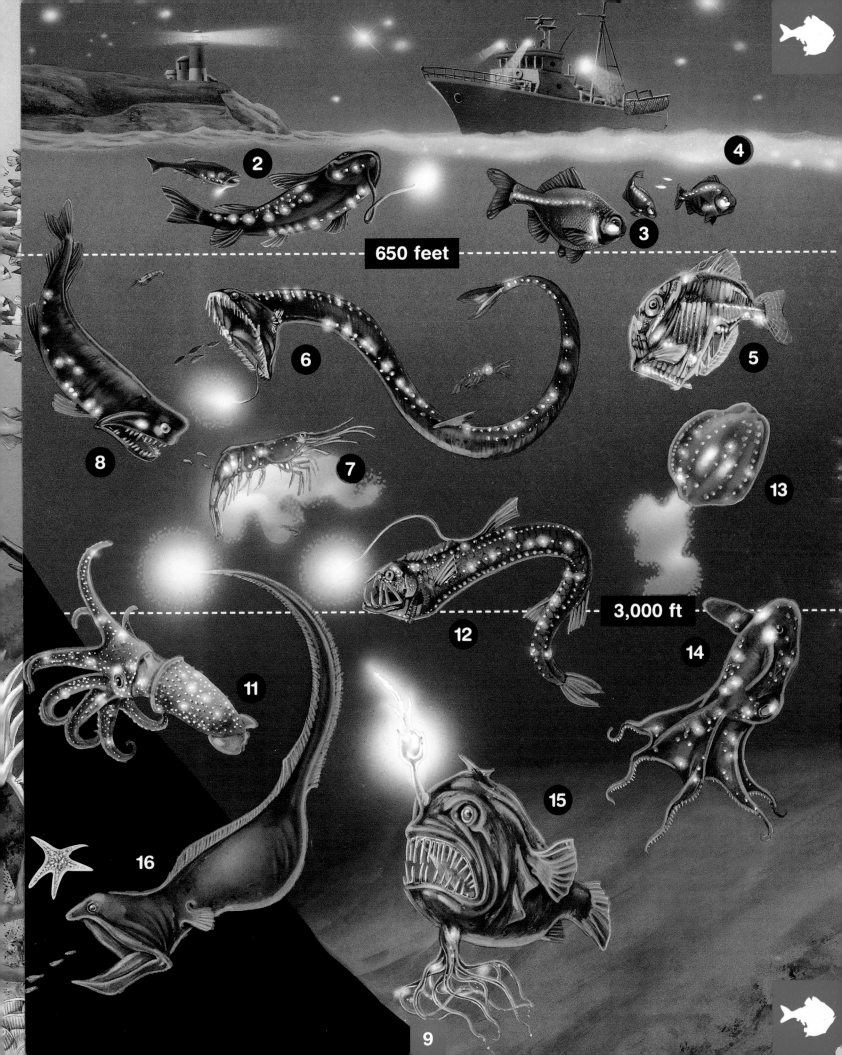

650 feet

3,000 ft

IN OCEAN waters more than 650 feet deep, very little light gets through. Only a few animals can live in the gloomy "twilight zone." Some, like the hatchetfish, the lantern fish, and the siphonophore (a kind of jellyfish), travel up to the surface at night to feed. The viperfish lurks in the murky depths. It uses its long teeth to stab its prey. The light on its back fin lures prey toward it.

Siphonophore

Lantern fish

Loosejaw

CREATURES OF THE TWILIGHT ZONE

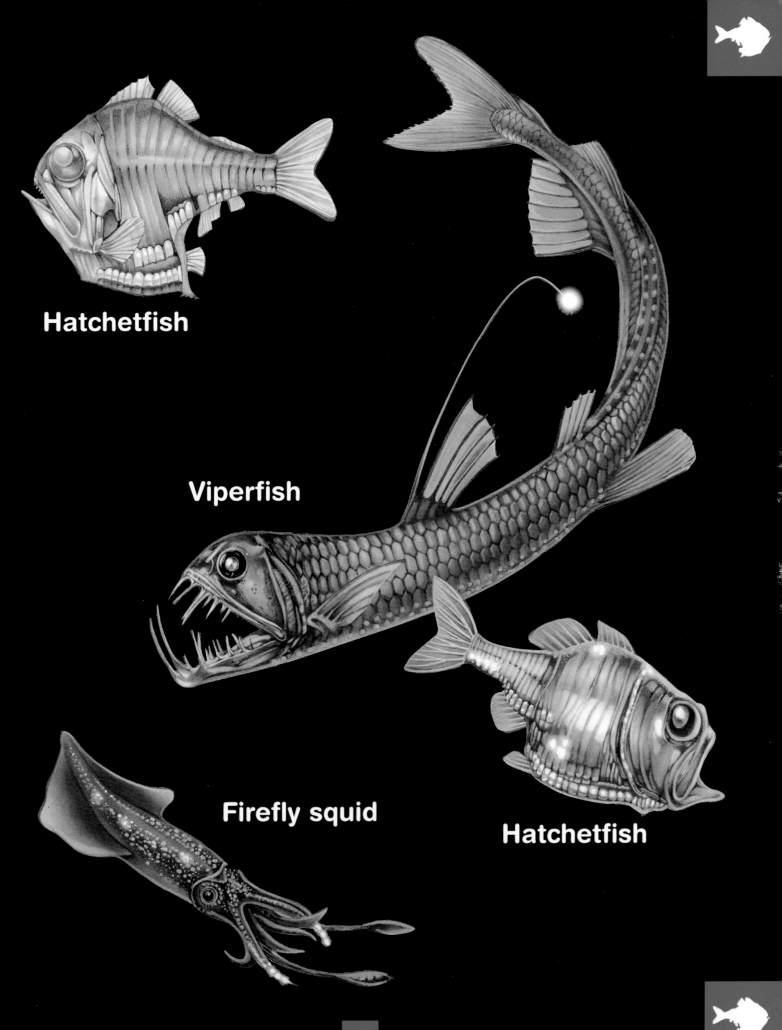

Hatchetfish

Viperfish

Firefly squid

Hatchetfish

Abyssal plain

Island

Continental shelf

Continental slope

IF THE WATERS of the oceans were drained away, the ocean floor would look like this. Most of it is a level plain called the abyssal plain. Around its edges there is a ledge called the continental shelf. Here the ocean bed slopes gently away from the land, before plunging down the steep continental slope to the abyssal plain.

THE OCEAN FLOOR

Ridge

Ocean trench

The abyssal plain is covered with steep-sided mountains. Some of them are so high that they poke up above the ocean waters to form islands. In tropical waters, coral reefs grow up close to the shores of these islands.

A long, jagged ridge rises from the abyssal plain. Its slopes have long cracks in them. Also winding across the plain is a deep gash called an ocean trench. Some ocean trenches plunge to more than 6 miles below the ocean surface.

SOME animals live in very deep ocean waters, more than 3,000 feet below the surface. No sunlight reaches these bitterly cold, still waters. But the water is aglow with light made by the animals themselves. The anglerfish and the gulper eels use their lights to catch small animals, drawn toward them by the glow. The vampire squid scares off its attackers by suddenly glowing.

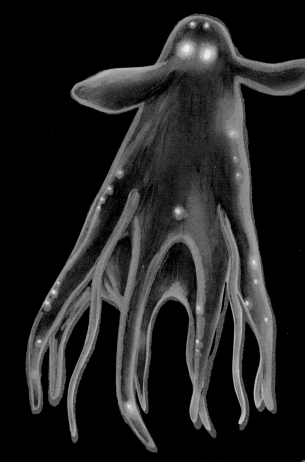

Vampire squid

GLOWING MONSTERS OF THE DEEP

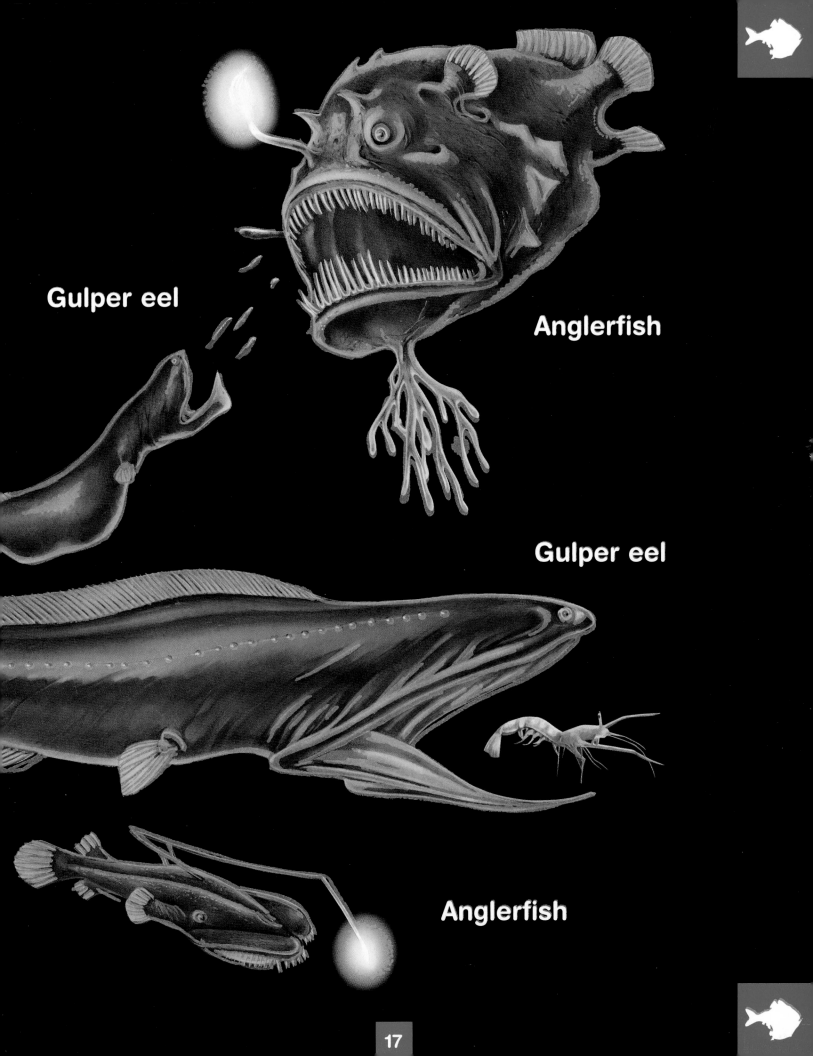

Gulper eel

Anglerfish

Gulper eel

Anglerfish

LIFE ON THE OCEAN FLOOR

WHAT LIVES on the deep ocean bed, thousands of feet below the surface? Here there is a vast, level plain of muddy "ooze." It is completely dark, icy cold, and deathly quiet.

Some ocean floor animals burrow in the ooze. Sea pens stand in it like plants, while sea cucumbers and spiders creep about. Tripod fish perch on their fins and wait for their prey.

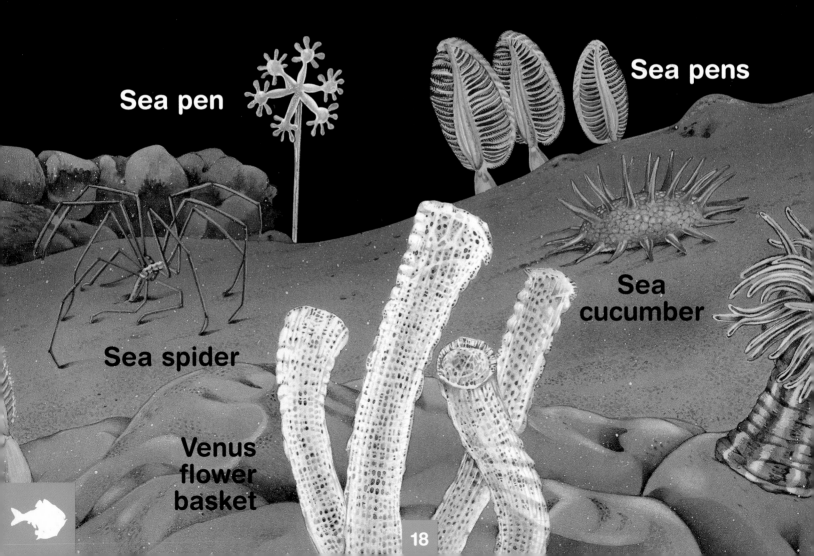

Sea pen

Sea pens

Sea spider

Sea cucumber

Venus flower basket

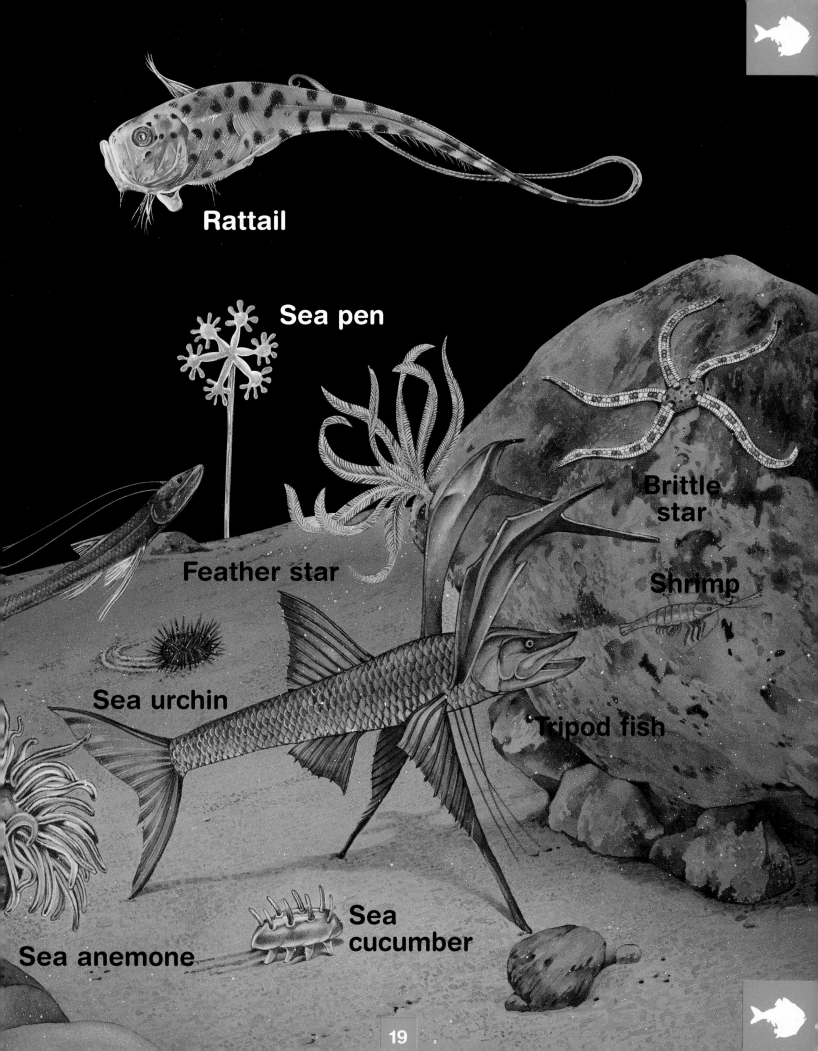

Rattail

Sea pen

Brittle
star

Feather star

Shrimp

Sea urchin

Tripod fish

Sea anemone

Sea
cucumber

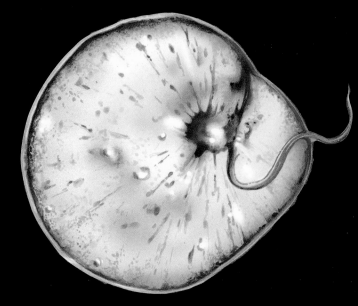

OCEAN waters are brimming with microscopic animals and plants called plankton. Dinoflagellates are plants. They have no roots and drift in the water. We can see their detailed shapes through a microscope. Many produce light. Ocean waters sometimes sparkle with the light of millions of dinoflagellates. Copepods are tiny crustaceans, related to crabs and shrimp.

MICROORGANISMS

**Copepod
(Gaussia Princeps)**
magnified 40 times

Dinoflagellate
(Noctiluca)
magnified 160 times

Dinoflagellate
(Pyrocystis)
magnified 160 times

Dinoflagellate
(Ceratocorys horrida)
magnified 1,000 times

Dinoflagellate
(Ceratium)
magnified 700 times

THE SPERM WHALE can dive to depths of 3,000 feet—and almost certainly deeper than that. It may spend up to two hours below water in search of its favorite prey, giant squid. No one has ever seen a sperm whale attack a giant squid, but it is probably a violent struggle.

Sperm whale

SPERM WHALE, CHAMPION DIVER

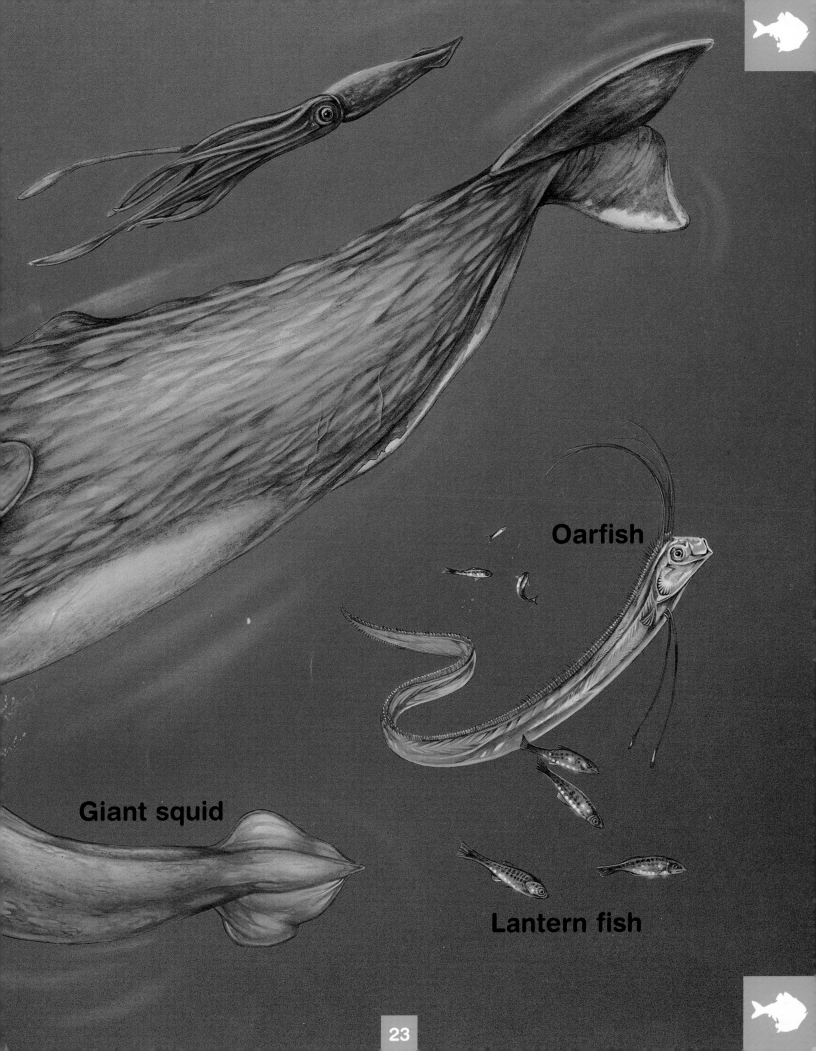

Oarfish

Giant squid

Lantern fish

Submersible

PEOPLE do not usually dive below 130 feet. The pressure of the water above is too great. But they can go much deeper in a submersible, protected inside its thick metal walls.

OCEAN EXPLORERS

Using lights and cameras on board a submersible, divers can find out about wrecks and ocean life. Robots may also be used to take pictures and gather samples.

Robot

Shipwreck

ABYSSAL PLAIN A large, flat area of the ocean floor. It lies between 13,000 and 20,000 feet below the ocean surface.

BATHYPELAGIC ZONE Ocean waters that lie at a depth of greater than about 3,000 feet. No sunlight reaches here.

BIOLUMINESCENCE The production of light by living things. It enables ocean creatures *(above right)* to find one another in the dark waters for mating, or to lure prey.

CONTINENTAL SHELF Part of the ocean floor near the edge of the continents. It lies no deeper than 650 feet below the water's surface.

CORAL REEF A stony bank found in shallow, tropical seas. It is made by many thousands of tiny animals called polyps.

USEFUL WORDS

CRUSTACEANS Animals that have hard outer skeletons and jointed legs. They include crabs, lobsters, and shrimp.

DINOFLAGELLATES Microscopic plants that drift on the surface of the water. Some glow in the dark.

OCEAN RIDGE A long mountain range that rises from the ocean floor.

OCEAN TRENCH A long, narrow, very deep valley in the ocean bed. It plunges to depths of between 20,000 and 36,000 feet.

PLANKTON Tiny plants and animals that drift in the surface waters of the oceans. They provide food for many other ocean animals.

POLLUTION The spoiling of a natural environment by humans.

SUBMERSIBLE An underwater vessel *(below)* used to explore the ocean depths.

OCEAN FACTS

A sea is an area of salt water that is at least partly enclosed by land. An ocean is a vast area of salt water that lies between the continents.

There are four great oceans: in order of size, the Pacific, Atlantic, Indian, and Arctic (some say the Southern Ocean, which surrounds Antarctica, is a fifth.) At 70 million square miles, the Pacific covers about one-third of the globe.

Why is the sea blue? Sunlight is made up of a range of different colors, called a spectrum. Blue light is scattered by seawater more easily than red, orange, or yellow light. It is also absorbed ("swallowed up") more slowly.

The Arabian Gulf, where the waters are quite shallow, is the warmest sea. Temperatures may reach 96°F in summer. Waters may be near to 32°F at great depths even in tropical waters.

The tallest mountain (Mauna Kea, Hawaii, 33,480 ft from base to summit), the deepest trench (Marianas Trench, Pacific Ocean, at one point 35,830 ft deep), and the longest mountain range (the Mid-Oceanic Ridge, 40,000 miles) are all found in the oceans.

The Great Barrier Reef, off northeastern Australia, is the largest natural feature on Earth. At 1,260 miles long, the reef is even visible from space.

The largest animal on Earth is the blue whale. It can reach up to 108 feet in length. A baby blue is about 23 feet long and as heavy as a hippopotamus.

The fastest creature in the ocean is probably the sailfish, which can reach speeds of over 60 mph.

The box jellyfish is probably the most venomous creature on Earth. One touch of its stinging tentacles can kill a person in four minutes.

The largest fish is the whale shark, a gentle plankton-eating creature which can grow up to nearly 60 feet long. The largest predatory fish is the great white shark, the largest of which may be up to 23 feet long.